S0-CFJ-724

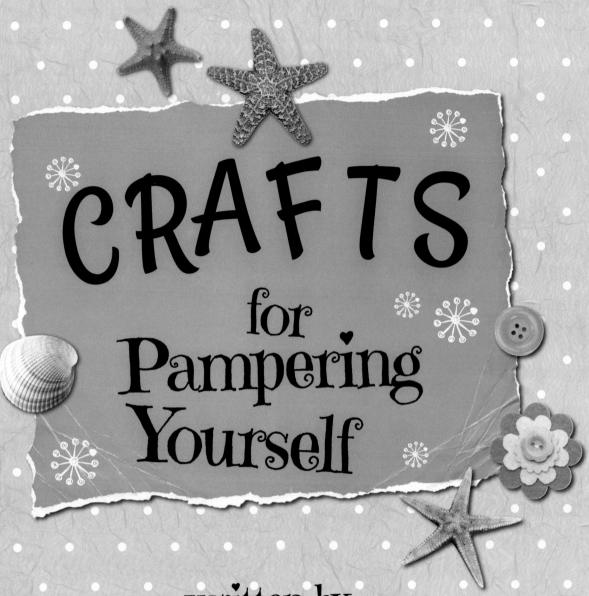

CRAFTS
for
Pampering
Yourself

written by
Susannah Blake

 Enslow Publishers, Inc.
40 Industrial Road
Box 398
Berkeley Heights, NJ 07922
USA
http://www.cnslow.com

This edition published by Enslow Publishers Inc.
All rights reserved.
No part of this book may be reproduced by any means without the written permission of the publisher.

Library of Congress Cataloging-in-Publication Data:

Blake, Susannah.
Crafts for pampering yourself /
Susannah Blake.
pages cm. — (Eco chic)
Audience: 9-12
Audience: Grade 4 to Grade 6
Summary: "A variety of crafts for kids to create their own face masks, bubbly bath bombs and shower pom-poms." —Provided by publisher
Includes bibliographical references.
ISBN 978-0-7660-4314-5
1. Handicrafts — Juvenile literature. 2. Recyling [Waste, etc.]
3. Gifts — Juvenile literature.
I. Title II. Series
TX 171.883 2013
745.5—dc23
2012025481

Future editions:
Paperback ISBN: 978-1-4644-0573-0

To Our Readers: We have done our best to make sure all Internet addresses in this book were active and appropriate when we went to press. However, the author and the publisher have no control over and assume no liability for the material available on those Internet sites or on other Web sites they may link to. Any comments or suggestions can be sent by e-mail to comments@enslow.com or to the address on the back cover.

Printed in China
122012 WKT, Shenzhen, Guangdong, China
10 9 8 7 6 5 4 3 2 1

First published in the UK in 2012 by Wayland
Copyright © Wayland 2012
Wayland
338 Euston Rd
London NW1 3BH

Editors: Julia Adams; Katie Woolley
Craft stylist: Annalees Lim
Designer: Rocket Design (East Anglia) Ltd
Photographer: Simon Pask, N1 Studios

Wayland is a division of Hachette Children's Books, an Hachette UK company.
www.hachette.co.uk

Picture acknowledgements:
All step-by-step and craft photography: Simon Pask, N1 Studios; images used throughout for creative graphics: Shutterstock.com

*Lavender bag
Page 18*

*Bath bomb
gift box
Page 24*

Contents

SAFETY ADVICE
When you make any of the projects in this book, always put safety first. Be extremely careful with sharp scissors, needles and pins and ask an adult if you need any help.

Learn stitches Page 30

Luscious lip balm Page 10

The Ugly Truth

Although we all love beauty products that make us feel pretty and pampered, there are some ugly facts behind them. The average pamper product contains a wealth of chemicals and substances that can harm the environment.

Many products such as soap, bubble bath, shampoo, body lotion, lipstick, eyeliner and hair gel all include ingredients derived from petroleum. Not only is petroleum a non-renewable resource, the products it is made into are not biodegradable and so cannot break down naturally. Another culprit is the antibacterial ingredients that are often found in soaps and cleansers. They do not break down in the environment and contribute to water pollution.

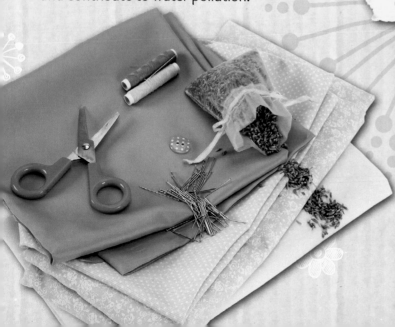

Packaging alert!

It's not just the lotions and potions we buy that can pose a threat to the environment. Stop for a moment and think about the packaging they come wrapped up in. Little feels so luxurious as a gorgeous new cleanser or bath milk in a shiny bottle nestled in a cardboard box, tied up with ribbon and shrink-wrapped in cellophane. But is all that packaging really necessary? Most of it is destined for the landfill site unless we choose to recycle, reclaim and reuse everything. And even if we do recycle, reclaim and reuse... do we really need all that packaging in the first place?

Making your own

It's incredibly easy to make your own beauty and pamper products at home and the benefits are obvious to see. By making your own, you avoid all the packaging waste that comes with commercial products. If you need containers to store products in, you can easily make beautiful ones yourself from reclaimed materials. When you make your own, you know what you have put into them. And by raiding the kitchen for ordinary ingredients you know that your product will be chemical-free (assuming you use organic ingredients) and biodegradable. Which is all good news for the environment!

Good news! You can make all these fab crafts from stuff that usually gets thrown out!

Make the right choices

When you buy products, always look at the label. Go for products that are organic, biodegradable and describe themselves as eco-friendly. Check that they are made from natural ingredients rather than chemicals. Choose products with the least packaging, and those packaged in recycled materials. Also make sure the products carry the recycle symbol so you know you can recycle them yourself once the product is finished.

Don't be trashy – recycle!

5

Wonderful wash bag

You will need

★ an old shower curtain
★ satin
★ scissors
★ needle and thread
★ 1 or 2 pretty buttons
★ ribbon or pretty cord

Make this super cool drawstring wash bag to keep all your beauty products in. Go pretty and practical using an old shower curtain for the main fabric, then line with more luxurious satin. If you can't find suitable fabric at home, look in secondhand and thrift stores. Lining fabric from an old coat is an ideal place to look for satin.

2 Place a square of satin on top of a square of shower curtain and sew the two together using a running stitch (see page 30). Repeat using the remaining two squares.

1 Cut two 9 in x 9 in squares from the shower curtain & two 8.5 in x 8.5 in squares from the satin.

Fruity face mask

This super-simple creamy face mask made with avocado, strawberries and honey will leave your skin smooth, soft and glowing.

Scoop the flesh from 1 avocado into a bowl, add three strawberries and mash together to make a smooth, creamy mixture. Stir in 1/2 tsp clear honey then smooth the mask over your face.

Sit back and relax for 10 minutes, then rinse off well with warm water and pat dry with a soft towel.

3

Cut out a decorative shape such as a heart or star from the remaining satin material and sew on to one of the shower curtain squares. You can add a few cute buttons, too.

4

Place the two squares together with the shower curtain sides facing each other. Sew along the sides and bottom, leaving a 1 in space at the top. Fold the top down and sew along the edge of the fabric to create a channel through which to thread the ribbon or cord.

Get ready for your next sleepover, your friends will love this!

5

Turn the bag inside out so the seams are on the inside. Thread one or two ribbons through each channel. Tie the ends of the ribbons at either side of the bag together in a knot.

Bath-tastic washcloth

You will need

★ two or three old towels
★ scissors
★ needle and thread
★ ribbon

Old towels can get pretty shabby after years of use. But with a bit of creative flair you can turn an old towel into a good-as-new washcloth! Simply cut your old towel into washcloth-sized squares and embellish pretty with a pretty trim and decorative shapes.

1

Cut an 7 in x 7 in square from one of the towels, as well as a star, less than a quarter of the size of the square.

2

Using running stitch (see page 30), sew the star onto a towel of a different color. Then cut around the star, leaving a 1/4 in border.

Rose and coconut bath soak

Make a fabulously luxurious bath soak out of simple ingredients from the kitchen. It has all the moisturizing, relaxing properties of a traditional bubble bath but none of the potential damaging effects of the soaps and chemicals many bubble baths contain. Run a bath, then add 1 tbsp rosewater and 1 tbsp coconut milk. Sit back and relax!

3

Use a whipstitch (see page 31) to attach the star to the square of towel.

4

Cut four strips from a towel, each 8 in long and 2 in wide. Ruffle each strip to fit the along a side of the towel square and attach it using a running stitch (see page 30).

The colors on this wash cloth could be reversed so it's dark with white edges. Why not make a contrasting set?

Luscious ♥ lip balm

Lip balm is easy to make yourself and it looks stunning stored in this pretty decorated pot. You'll need an extra-small container, so look out for old lip balm pots or tiny jars used for make up samples. An old eye shadow container could also be ideal. Just make sure you clean and dry the container really well before you fill it with the lip balm mixture.

You will need

For the pot:
- ★ scrap paper
- ★ scissors
- ★ double-sided tape
- ★ small pot
- ★ PVA glue
- ★ button

For the lip balm:
- ★ small saucepan
- ★ heatproof bowl (that will sit on top of the pan)
- ★ 1 tbsp beeswax
- ★ 1 tbsp olive oil
- ★ 1 tbsp clear honey

2

Stick the strips of paper onto the container lid. Cut short pieces off the strips to stick onto the side of the container.

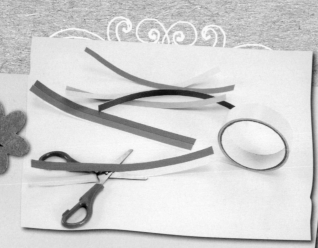

1

Choose some brightly colored pages from magazines or colorful pieces of scrap paper. Cut about 10-12 narrow strips and stick them onto double-sided tape.

Lip balm

Pour about 2 in of water into the saucepan. Place the bowl on top, making sure it doesn't touch the water. Put the beeswax, oil and honey in the bowl. Put the pan with the bowl on the stove. Heat gently until the ingredients have melted. Stir well to combine, then pour into your lip balm pot. Leave to set. Use within three months.

3

Take care when heating the lip balm ingredients – they get very hot. You may want to ask an adult to help you.

Cut petal shapes out of the scrap paper or magazine pages. You can stick slightly smaller petals onto slightly larger ones for a layered effect.

4

Stick the petals together to form a flower and glue the button in the middle. When the flower has dried, stick it onto the lid of the container. Curl the tips of the petals up.

Why not add a drop of vanilla essence to your lip balm mixture to give it a delicious scent!

Perfumed potpourri

A bowl of gorgeously scented potpourri looks really pretty on any dressing table or bathroom window sill and will make the air sweet and fragrant. Make this funky bowl from scratch out of papier mâché, then fill it with your very own homemade potpourri. Using natural essential oils is much better for the environment than toxic, non-biodegradable chemicals.

Wood shavings

You may be able to find wood shavings at your local lumberyard. Ask for a bagful or two. There should be plenty on the floor that they'll be happy to give away. Or you may be able to find them at a pet store. Wood shavings are used for animal bedding.

You will need

★ balloon
★ PVA glue
★ tissue paper
★ scissors
★ paintbrush
★ the cardboard ring from a roll of packing tape
★ wood shavings and/or dried flower petals and dried twigs
★ scented oil, such as rose or lavender

1 Blow up the balloon and tie a knot in it. Mix 3 parts PVA glue with 1 part water.

2 Cut the tissue paper into pretty shapes. You will need many sheets' worth of shapes, so you might want to fold the tissue paper a few times before cutting out a shape.

3

Place the balloon upright into a glass or cup. Apply glue to the shapes and stick them onto the rounded half of the balloon. Apply at least three layers of the shapes.

4

Place the cardboard ring onto the top of the balloon. Attach it by sticking strips of tissue around its inside and outside edges. Once the papier mâché is dry, burst the balloon and remove it.

Potpourri was used in France as long ago as the 17th century! Ingredients used included cedar, cinnamon, cloves, juniper and lavender.

5

Fill a plastic bag with the wood shavings or petals, add scented oil and shake the bag to spread the mixture. Then place your potpourri in your funky bowl!

Pampering pom-pom

This groovy bath pom-pom is a must for every girl's shower or bath. Use it to gently rub over your skin to exfoliate and leave you with glowing arms and legs. Rinse after use and you can use it again and again! You can reuse old net curtains or netting from an underskirt to make the pom-pom. If you don't have anything suitable at home, take a trip to your local thrift store.

You will need

★ netting
★ scissors
★ needle and thread
★ 12 in pretty cord or ribbon

1

Cut the netting into about twelve 2 in x 12 in rectangles.

2

Fold each rectangle in half and stack them, alternating the side on which you place the folded edge.

3

Using needle and thread, firmly stitch the layers together in the center of the rectangles.

4

Tie the cord or ribbon around the middle of the rectangles, pulling very tightly and knotting well. Tie the end of the cord or ribbon together to make a loop. Then fluff the netting to create the pom-pom shape.

This pom-pom makes a fab present for your friends, too!

Make your own body scrub

Get smooth, tingling skin using this simple mixture of kitchen ingredients. It's perfect for the summer when you're wearing shorts and T-shirts and want your skin to look at its best. Sea salt is a natural exfoliant, while ginger warms and improves circulation and olive oil gently moisturizes.

Put 2 tbsp sea salt, 1 tbsp grated fresh root ginger, grated rind of 1 lemon, 1/4 peeled cucumber and 1 tbsp olive oil in a blender. Blend together then gently rub onto your legs or arms in a circular motion. Rinse off with warm water and pat dry.

Homemade hair gel

You will need

For the pot:
- ★ blue and purple tissue paper
- ★ scissors
- ★ PVA glue
- ★ clean, empty pot with lid
- ★ paintbrush
- ★ glitter glue

For the hair gel:
- ★ 1 tsp gelatin
- ★ 1 cup warm water
- ★ peppermint oil

Create your own salon style with this very cool and very simple homemade hair gel. You even get to make a customized pot for it! Store the hair gel in the fridge and use within a week.

1

Cut the purple tissue paper into wave shapes and cut small squares out of the blue tissue paper.

2

Glue the shapes onto the side of the pot using the PVA glue and a paintbrush. Wash the paintbrush as soon as you have finished.

Why not make pretty customized pots for your store-bought cosmetics, too?

3

Peppermint hair gel

Stir the gelatin into the warm water until completely dissolved. If you want a scented hair gel, add 2-3 drops of peppermint oil to the mixture. Pour the mixture into the customized pot and chill in the fridge for about five hours until set.

Tear up blue tissue paper into small pieces and soak in cold water for about an hour until it's very soft. Squeeze out most of the water, then mix in just enough PVA glue to make a thick, doughy paste. Mold the paste into a wave shape and leave to dry.

4

Glue the wave to the pot lid and decorate with glitter glue.

Lavender bag

You will need

You will need

★ pretty fabrics
★ scissors
★ needle and thread
★ dried lavender
★ small funnel
★ ribbon
★ pretty button

Hang this scented lavender bag on a hanger in your wardrobe to make your clothes smell divine! Choose pretty fabrics from an old dress, shirt or skirt, and look out for ribbon from cosmetics packaging.

1 Using the fabrics, cut out two heart shapes (about 4 1/2 in wide), two bird shapes (one slightly smaller than the other) and a wing shape.

2 Using a whipstitch (see page 31), sew the bird shapes onto one of the hearts and the wing shape onto the bird.

How to dry lavender
Lavender has a beautiful, strong fragrance and is ideal for drying. If you have a lavender bush at home, simply pluck off some of the flower heads and arrange on a baking sheet. Leave in a warm dry place such as a sunny windowsill to dry completely. If you don't have your own fresh lavender to dry, you can buy dried lavender from health food stores.

Lavender is easy to grow. If you don't have a garden, you can grow it indoors in a pot, too.

3

Place the two heart shapes together, with the patterned sides facing each other. Using a running stitch (see page 30), sew around the edge of the hearts leaving a 3/4 in gap on one side.

4

Turn the heart inside out, and use the funnel to fill it with lavender. Sew up the open edge.

5

Fold the ribbon, then sew the ends to the top of the heart. You can also tie a short piece of ribbon around the bottom of the loop in a bow. Sew the button to the bird, positioning it as its eye.

Funky fish soap dish

You will need

★ foam sheets in various colours
★ scissors
★ pen
★ craft glue (make sure it's suitable for glueing plastic)
★ 2 used CDs
★ 4 old dice

It can be hard to think of a good use for old CDs, but here's a great way to keep them out of the garbage! They're shiny, waterproof and round- just perfect for turning into a glitzy, cute soap dish with a fishy theme.

1 Draw the shapes for your fish (fins, tail, mouth and eyes) onto the foam sheets. Using a CD as a template, draw a ring that has a .5 in border. Cut all the shapes out.

2 Stick some small squares of foam onto the ring. Then stick the fins, tail and mouth onto one of the CDs. Stick the ring, eyes and any other shapes you want on the top of the soap dish onto the other CD.

Make your own soap

Instead of throwing out those tiny nubs of soap that are always leftover from a bar, save them up in a jar ready to turn into a whole new bar!

To make your own soap, make sure your scraps of soap are dry. Grate them into a bowl, then add 1 tsp water at a time, stirring well until the mixture becomes soft enough to press into a ball. If the mixture is crumbly you need a little more water; if it is too soft, grate in a little more soap. Shape the mixture and leave to dry for a week before using.

3

Stick the decorated discs together, so that the fin, mouth and tail shapes are between the two CDs.

4

Stick the four dice to the bottom CD.

We used groovy dice for the feet, but cut up corks will work well, too.

Why not try different animal themes for your soap dish? How about an octopus or a shark?

A bath infusion

Bubble bath alert!

Many traditional bath products are made from ingredients derived from petroleum. They don't break down when you let your bath water drain away and can cause damage to the environment.

Make sure your bathing stays eco-friendly by choosing organic products that use natural, plant-based ingredients. Even better, make your own products using naturally grown foods like this bath infusion.

These pretty bags, filled with fragrant herbs known for their relaxing properties, are a wonderful, natural way to scent your bath water. Once you've used the bag, simply empty the herbs into the compost, rinse out the bag and leave to dry, ready to fill with more herbs when the mood takes. You can use old net curtains, very thin cotton or an old baby muslin to make the bags.

You will need

For the bags:
* cardboard
* paper plate
* thin cotton or muslin
* scissors
* needle and thread
* ribbon

For the infusion:
* 1 tbsp dried lavender flowers
* 1 tbsp dried chamomile flowers

1 Place the paper plate on the cardboard and draw around it. Cut out the shape to use as a template.

2 Use the template to draw four circles on the muslin or cotton.

3

Cut the circles out.

4

Fold the edge of each circle inwards and use a running stitch (see page 30) to create a hem of about .75 in.

For a relaxing bath, add a fragrance bag to the hot water, plus a cup of milk.

5

Thread ribbon onto a needle and thread it through the 'channel' of the hem. Fill each bag with dried chamomile and lavender flowers and draw closed with the ribbon.

Bath bomb gift box

Make these fantastic fizzing bath bombs using everyday kitchen ingredients, which makes them environmentally friendly as well as fun to use! You will be able to find most of the ingredients in health food stores. Your bath bombs will make beautiful gifts, wrapped up in this fab gift box.

You will need

For the gift box:

★ tracing paper or greaseproof baking paper
★ thin cardboard
★ ruler
★ scissors
★ used wrapping paper
★ glue
★ ribbon

For the bath bombs:

★ 1 cup baking soda
★ 1/2 cup citric acid
★ large glass or ceramic bowl
★ spoon
★ essential oil, such as peppermint, lavender or rose
★ 1-2 tsp vegetable oil
★ spray bottle filled with water
★ mold, such as heart-shaped ice cube tray or small yogurt container

1 Using tracing paper, transfer the shape of the template at the back of this book onto the cardboard.

2 Score the folds (dotted lines on the template), using the ruler and a dried up ball point pen. This will make the box easier to fold. Then cut out the shape and stick it onto the wrapping paper. Trim the wrapping paper.

3

Fold the box and stick the sides together using glue.

Bath bombs

Combine the baking soda and citric acid in the bowl. Add about 10 drops of essential oil and the vegetable oil and stir well. Spray a tiny bit of water over the mixture and stir well. Continue gradually adding a spritz of water and stirring until the mixture has a soft and doughy consistency. Press the mixture into the molds and leave to dry until hard. Then pop them into your gift box!

Why not try adding a little glitter to the bath bombs— sparkle-tastic!

4

Fold the base of the box as shown in the picture below. Tie the ribbon around your box for a pretty finishing touch.

Groovy grooming!

You will need

- ★ cardboard cereal box
- ★ ruler
- ★ scissors
- ★ fabric
- ★ double-sided sticky tape
- ★ pins
- ★ needle and thread
- ★ ribbon
- ★ 8 buttons

Make your own vanity kit and store it in this clever folding vanity tray! Use fabric from an old dress or skirt or an old curtain to make the vanity tray. You can also upcycle your old hairbrush with a lick of paint and some sequins from old clothes.

2

Cut out a rectangle of fabric about 12.5 in x 14 in. Place the large rectangle in the center and arrange the smaller rectangles along each edge leaving a .25 in gap between each rectangle. Stick the rectangles onto the fabric, using the double-sided tape.

1

On the cereal box, mark one 5.5 in x 8 in rectangle; two 3.25 in x 5.5 in rectangles; and two 3 in x 8 in rectangles. Cut them out.

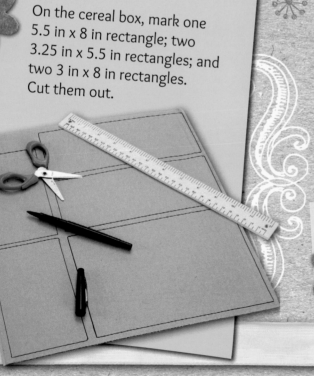

3

Place another rectangle of fabric (also measuring 12.5 in x 14 in) over the cardboard pieces. Use pins to attach the top fabric to the bottom one.

26

4

Use a whipstitch (see page 31) around the edges to sew the two fabric rectangles together. Then use a running stitch (see page 30) to sew along the gaps between the cardboard rectangles.

5

Sew the end of a piece of ribbon (about 7 in long) to the spots where each running stitch seam meets the edge of the fabric. You can also sew a button onto the ribbon to add a pretty finish. Then fold up the sides of the tray and tie the ribbons together at the corners.

To upcycle your old brush, use left-over paint and stick on some sequins when the paint has dried.

Throw a pamper party

W hether you're spoiling your mom and giving her a pamper treat, or inviting your friends to recreate a spa experience—there's no end to the fun you can have with eco-friendly, homemade pamper products.

Soothe your senses!

Create a salon in your own home

Before you offer your own home spa experience, do a bit of planning. First of all, think about who you want to pamper. Then think about the kind of pampering they'd like.

If it's your mom, she might really enjoy a bit of peace and quiet, so how about running her a hot bath and giving her the choice of a rose and coconut bath soak (page 8) or relaxing bath infusion (pages 22-23). Make sure the bathroom's really clean and tidy, then organize some relaxing music, maybe some dim lighting or candles (although check she's happy with you lighting candles before you do!), a relaxing cup of tea, a magazine and then leave her to soak in your homemade scented bath.

If you want to entertain your friends, they might enjoy having a group facial and manicure. You could whiz up the facial in the kitchen together, then help each other apply the mask before you sit back and file your nails while the treatment works its magic!

Alternatively, you could create a real spa experience. Create a "Treatment List" on pretty paper so that your friends can choose the products they'd like. Then it's up to you to play beautician, mixing up the products and applying them while your friends enjoy the pampering.

The wash bag (pages 6–7) could make a cute party beauty bag

Party packs

If you're throwing a party for friends, why not put together some beauty bags for them to take home? Dry products such as bath bombs, soap or scented infusion bags make ideal gifts. Reuse pretty gift boxes or bags and tie them with ribbon to really make an impact. Alternatively, make your own gift boxes or bags from old wrapping paper and reused ribbon.

Craft skills

How to thread a needle

Cut a length of thread. Make sure it is no longer than your arm; too long a piece of thread will become knotted and make sewing hard work. Pass the tip of the thread through the eye of the needle. If the ends are frayed, dampen them slightly. Hold the two ends of thread together and loop into a knot. Doubling up the thread will help to make your sewing stronger.

Starting and finishing a line of stitching

To start, fasten the thread to the fabric using a few backstitches. End a line of tacking with one backstitch or a knot.

Sewing on buttons

Buttons usually have two or four holes, or have a single loop underneath. They need to be sewn on very firmly with plenty of stitches as they are generally subject to lots of wear and tear.

For a two-hole or looped button, sew through the holes or loop on to the fabric about six times in the same direction. Tie off on the underside of the fabric. For a four-hole button, use the same technique as for the two-hole button, using opposite holes to make a cross pattern.

Tacking stitch

This is used to hold the fabric in position while it is being permanently stitched and is ideal for gathering fabric into ruffles. Pass the needle in and out of the fabric in a line to make long, even stitches.

To make ruffles, do not tie off the line of stitching, Gently pull the thread, sliding the fabric together into gathers or ruffles. When you have created the desired effect, tie off with a backstitch or knot.

Running stitch

Similar to the tacking stitch, the running stitch uses smaller stitches. It is used for seams and for gathering and can also be used to decorative effect, particularly with wool or embroidery thread. You can stitch lines or curling patterns onto the surface of fabric.

Pass the needle in and out of the fabric in small, even stitches.

Whipstitch

This stitch is used to secure two pieces of fabric together at the edges.

Place two pieces of fabric on top of each other.

Fasten the thread to the inside of one piece of fabric. Pass the needle through both pieces of fabric from underneath, passing through where you have fastened the thread. Stitch through from the underside again to make a diagonal stitch about .25 in from the first stitch.

Blanket stitch

This is a decorative stitch used to bind the edge of fabric. Use a contrasting coloured thread for maximum effect.

Fasten the thread on the underside of the fabric, then pass the needle from the underside. Make a looped stitch over the edge of the fabric but before you pull it tight, pass the needle through the loop. Repeat.

Glossary

accessory: a fashion item, such as jewelry, a scarf or a bag, that can be added to enhance your overall fashion look

biodegradable: describes materials or substances that can be decomposed by natural bacteria

consumer: a person who buys products and services for personal use

contaminant: a toxic or poisonous substance that infects or dirties other substances

decompose: the process by which man-made and natural materials and substances break down. It can be another word for rotting.

Eco: short for ecology; sometimes used in front of words to imply a positive effect on the environment, for example 'eco fashion'

environment: the natural world, including air, soil, water, plants, and animals

landfill: also known as a dump, a landfill is a site used for the disposal of waste materials

organic: plants and animals that are grown or reared entirely naturally without the use of synthetic inputs such as pesticides, fertilizers and antibiotics

pesticide: a chemical used to prevent, destroy or repel pests

pollution: the release of environmental contaminants

recycle: to use something again, usually after processing or remaking in some way

toxic: poisonous

trend: popular fashion or style at a given time

upcycle: to take something that is disposable and transform it into something of greater use and value

Useful websites

freecycle.org: a website helping to keep unwanted consumer goods out of a landfill. It brings together people who want to get rid of things and people who need those things.

etsy.com: a website where people can buy and sell handmade crafts. A great source for craft inspiration.

folksy.com: a website where people can buy, sell and learn how to make handmade crafts.

Index